Let's Move

LET'S MOVE

Enjoyable Physical Activities and Games
for Children between the Ages of 3 and 7

Book 2

ANIMALS – ANIMALS – ANIMALS

Meyer & Meyer Sport

Editor: Heidi Lindner, Pipo-Lernwerkstatt, Neumünster
Authors: Gisela Stein, Heidi Lindner
Illustrations: Silke Mehler
Translation coordination: Gisela Stein
Translated by Jean Wanko

Animals, Animals, Animals/ed. by Heidi Lindner
-Oxford: Meyer & Meyer Sport (UK) Ltd., 2002
(Let's Move: 2)
ISBN 1-84126-065-7

Aachen, Adelaide, Auckland, Budapest, Graz, Johannesburg, Miami, Olten (CH), Oxford, Singapore, Toronto
Member of the World
Sports Publishers' Association
www.w-s-p-a.org

Printed in Germany by Druckpunkt Offset GmbH, Bergheim
ISBN 1-84126-065-7
E-Mail: verlag@meyer-meyer-sports.com
www.meyer-meyer-sports.com

Publisher's Statement

The games and exercises described in this book have been tried and tested many times, without any problems, by the authors and the children in their care. However, teachers, parents and any other adults using this book for source material must ensure that the children in their care play within a safe and secure enviroment. The publisher cannot be held liable should accidents occur. Correct and standard procedures on health and safety should be followed at all times.

CONTENTS

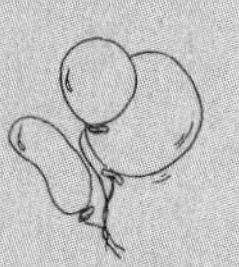

Dear Readers,

This time we're going to have animals creeping and crawling, hopping, swimming and flying through the various areas of our series "**Let's Move**".

By using our ideas, we should like to encourage nursery and playschool teachers, preschool and elementary school teachers and the children themselves to sing, play and move about together; and so we're offering a wide range of activities both inside and outside, giving groups of children suitable forms of exercise to which they can enjoy moving around and which will lead into other basic forms of sport due to their wide scope of movement.

The main point of emphasis drawn from the children's own surroundings runs as a recurring theme through the practical areas.

By using finger games and easily recognizable songs we relate to the smallest children and create a relaxed and trusting atmosphere. This helps to get rid of any fears and inhibitions quickly and can also be repeated at home. As well as all the movement offered at nursery and elementary school, children will find in our "Pieces of usual and unusual small apparatus" section all sorts of ideas for playing at home, with their families and in their leisure time. "Stories to move to" are aimed at encouraging the children to use their imagination in a wide variety of movements, thus extending their own personal repertoire. A resourceful and creative teacher, willing to try out new ideas, can create an unlimited field of practice just by telling stories.

In the area of "Small Games", we've collected together some ideas which can be introduced without too much fuss and bother. They are also suitable for bridging gaps between one section and another. For "Fun Activities" like parties and hikes, which further group community feeling, we need to call on each leader's imagination and creativity, but we are offering you a few incentives as to how you can organize such events. In the "Creative Corner" you will find our instructions for making and building things as well as plans you can copy.

Each group leader will undoubtedly find her own main themes as she works with the children, and they in turn will collect different ideas for movement by linking the various areas of practice, together, which furthers their mobility skills as well as developing their whole personality. The top priority is to really enjoy moving about.

So – off we go; let's try and slide into the skin or under the fur of animals and have an incredibly good time.

Yours, *Gisela Stein, Heidi Lindner* and *Silke Mehler*

Finger Games and Songs

We all know that it is fun to sing, but nowadays families are singing together less and less. Singing as well as games and movements presented to a circle of children create a relaxed atmosphere within the group. They help withdrawn and shy children as well as newcomers get rid of their fears and inhibitions more quickly. The children's imagination is challenged to adopt the exercise leader's songs, ideas for playing and individual programmes. They can then easily take these singing and playing ideas home with them as well as bringing new songs back to the sports hall with them next time. I'm sure you all know some suitable songs or music and movement games which would fit our "animals" theme!

The Mouse Family

The story of the mouse family is a finger puppet game that can be played with tiny children if not with babies. Fathers and mothers take their children onto their laps and play the finger puppet game with the child's hand. Please ensure that the narrator leaves enough time in between each line for the children to copy the movements.

This is daddy mouse,
Show me one thumb.

And he looks just like all other mice,
Wiggle your thumb.

He's got a soft little coat,
Use your left hand to stroke the back of your right hand

and su-u-u-u-ch a long tail.
Stretch your hands out to show how long his tail is.

He's got a little pointed nose,
Move your thumbs and fingers towards each other to make a nose.

and two little ears above it.
Stretch out your first and middle finger, hiding you thumb behind your ring finger.

He's got teeth to bite with,
Bend your fingers to make biting movements, moving the tips of your fingers towards each other.

and feet for running away with.
Your finger crawl away from your body maybe up your arms or down your legs.

As children often shout out "more, more", you could introduce the other members of the mouse family, using your first finger, middle finger, ring finger and little finger in turn to play each mouse.

I'm sure you can think up a wide range of relatives as well as mother, grandma, grandpa, auntie, uncle, little Charlie and baby mouse.

But remember! Grandma and grandpa have probably lost all their front teeth, and that the baby mouse's tail is a lot shorter than the grown-up mice!

As with all finger puppet games, you can also turn these into movement games. Then the various members of the family are introduced as in a pantomime and, when they hear the word "run away", some children run off, some try to catch them again.

THE EASILY FRIGHTENED LITTLE MOUSE

One afternoon a little grey mouse
came carefully out of its little mouse house.

Bring the thumb of your right hand to the four remaining fingers to form a mouse nose. Form with the left hand a roof above it, which indicates the little "mouse house".

Move your thumb and fingers towards each other.

It cautiously peered to the left and the right

Scurry with your index- and middlefinger to the right and the left side without caring about the left hand.

sniffing eagerly to its heart's delight.

Lay your right hand flat on surface.

It hoped to find a great big piece
of delicious-tasting cheddar cheese.

Scurry with your index- and middlefinger quickly to and fro.

With a wiggly nose it searched around

Scurrying as well, but remaining still now and again.

when suddenly there was a terrible sound!

Hold your fingers quite still.

Alarmed it scurried as fast as a mouse....

Run away very fast

....can scurry into its nice little house.

under your left hand, which is reforming
a mouse house.

By the way: You can turn this fingerplay into
an action game for the classroom or playground as well.

THE FIVE DIFFERENT FINGERS

Tommy Thumb, Tommy Thumb,
where are you? Where are you?
Hello and good morning, hello and good morning.
I will go! I will go!

Peter Pointer, Peter Pointer,
where are you? Where are you?
Hello and good morning, hello and good morning.
I will go! I will go!

Tony Tall, Tony Tall,
where are you? Where are you?
Hello and good morning, hello and good morning.
I will go! I will go!

Bobby Ring, Bobby Ring,
where are you? Where are you?
Hello and good morning, hello and good morning.
I will go! I will go!

Baby Small, Baby Small,
where are you? Where are you?
Hello and good morning, hello and good morning.
I will go! I will go!

Fingers all, Fingers all,
where are you? Where are you?
Hello and good morning, hello and good morning.
We will go! We will go!

GAME IDEA:

All children are sitting in a circle on the floor hiding their hands behind their backs. They bring first one hand and then the other to the fore. To the text "Hello and good Morning" they snap the thumbs till "I will go" at which point the children hide their hands again behind the backs. In like manner the other fingers appaer and disappear with "I will go".

We are running, yes, we are

We are running, yes, we are,
yes, we are,
yes, we are.
We are running, yes, we are,
we are running.

We are stamping, yes, we are,
yes, we are,
yes, we are.
We are stamping, yes, we are,
we are stamping.

We are clapping ....
We are hopping ....
We are jumping ....
We are dancing ...
We are waving ...
and what else?

Five Little Fishes

Swish, swosh, swishy, swoshy,
Swish, swosh, swishy, swoshy.

5 little fish were swimming in the sea,
and one of them said:
"I don't like this any more;
I'd far rather be in a little pond,
'cos a shark's swimming round,
and he'll gobble me up.

4 little fish…
3 little fish…
2 little fish…

One little fish was swimming in the sea,
he said to himself:
"I don't like this anymore; ....etc.

One big shark was swimming in the sea,
he said to himself:
"I don't like this anymore;
I'd far rather be in a little pond,
where lots of fish are swimming round,
and I can gobble them all up."

GAME IDEA:

(You can make this text into a rap song!)

5 little fish where swimming in the sea, And one of them said: "I don't like this anymore,"	*(Hold up 5 fingers, do some breaststroke movements and then indicate the sea by making big wave movements with both hands.)*
I'd far rather be in a little pond, 'Cos a shark's swimming round	*(Indicate a pond with both hands; then let both hands wave apart from each other.)*
And he'll soon gobble me up.	*(When you hear "up", do a big hand clap in front of you.*
Swish, swosh, swishy, swoshy	*(Slap your right and left leg alternately with both hands.)*

5 little monkeys were sitting in a tree,
laughing at a crocodile,
you can't catch me!

(Movements: Move all five fingers of your right or left hand, followed by a throwing away movement.)

But then came the crocodile,
Snip, snip, snap
Snip, snip, snap

(Put both hands together at your wrist and make opening and closing snapping movements.)

4 little monkeys... (move only 4 fingers)
3 little monkeys... (as above)
2 little monkeys... (as above)

1 little monkey... (As above)

There were no little monkeys sitting in the tree
Hide your hands.

Laughing at a crocodile:
"You can't catch me, you can't catch me"
Shake your hands.

But then came the crocodile:
"burp, burp, burp..."
Put both hands together at your wrist again making a huge mouth and open it as wide as possible for the last burp.

5 little monkeys were sitting in a tree....
The game starts all over again

This little rhyme should be spoken rhythmically and accentuated as much as possible, so that the difference in speed of movement between the monkeys and the lumbering crocodile can be made clear by slow or fast speaking.

GAME IDEA 2:

This story can be made much more active if the children dress up and play hide-and-seek. The "catcher" crocodile has a large sheet over him under which the monkeys which he has caught gradually disappear. When he burps, they can step out from under the sheet and a new crocodile can start chasing monkeys.

The Tongue Mouse – A cheeky little mouse

Little three-year-old Laura, herself a cheeky little mouse, will now show us some tongue acrobatics which she learnt at nursery school.

A cheeky little mouse,
is looking out of her house,
she's looking left,
she's looking right,
she's looking up,
she's looking down,
she's looking round and round.
Then the cat creeps round the house,
the mouse scurries home,
sits and shakes so terribly;
then when the cat has disappeared,
the mouse lets out a great big shout:
Yippee-ee-ee!

A FLIGHT OF RELAXATION:

THE FLYING CARPET

Fantastic Airlines is offering a flight on flying carpets on which all our group members are invited. Our destinations are called dreams, relaxation and recovery. We don't need anything for our journey other than a soft mat, lots of peace and quiet, together with our imaginations and the ability to listen and follow our narrator. To help little children relax, adults can lie down with them on the mat, hold them in their arms and stroke them gently.

There's a brightly coloured carpet lying in the meadow. You can get on it and shut your eyes. The carpet floats gently up from the ground and floats higher and higher. Up above you, the sky is bright blue with only a few fluffy white clouds. A tiny, little breeze helps your carpet along.

Now you're gradually landing on your carpet in a wonderful flower garden –what a fantastic smell!

Butterflies are flying around, flapping from one flower to another. Big trees wave their branches gently to and fro in the winds. You can hear some quiet tweeting and a fountain splashing.

Then your carpet floats back in the air and your dream journey continuous. You're flying slowly, floating along as you see the sky shining above you. The sun is warming your skin and you feel good. Now you're about to land again.

Your carpet has arrived on a white sandy beach. You can see the sea, the waves and the foaming crests of the waves. Sunbeams are twinkling and dancing on the surface of the water and boats are sailing by. A beautifully coloured flag is waving on the beach.

Yet again, your carpet is rising in the air and we're slowly flying home. Sadly, your dream journey is nearly over. We land, rub our eyes and are surprised to find ourselves back in the sports hall.

Perception

Alongside opportunities for satisfying their need to move around, children also need times of rest and relaxation in order to develop healthily both mentally and physically. For this reason, readers and exercise leaders should incorporate children's relaxation stories from time to time in their lesson programme.

During the "relaxation stories for your back", which can also be done in pairs, it's important to ensure that children enjoy engaging in body contact. If a child should refuse, he/she shouldn't be forced to do it, but rather watch and listen to the other children working.

We should like to point out at this stage that the vertebral column (backbone) should be left out of all back massage, so that no health risks occur by too much pressure on the vertebral discs.

Let's Buy an Animal

The children work together in pairs, with one lying on his/her tummy on a soft mat, whilst the other kneels alongside.

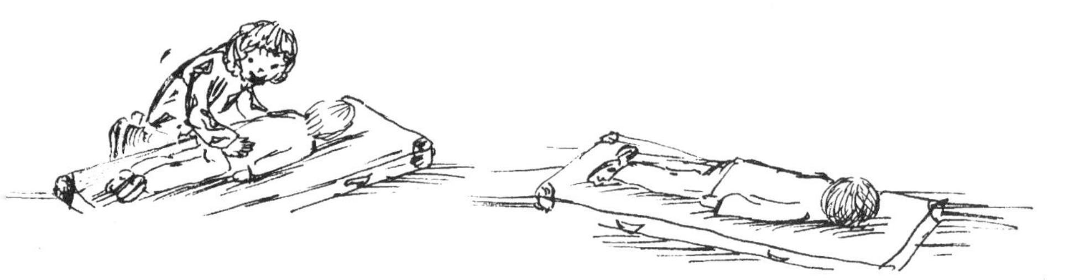

Whilst the story is being told, there should be complete silence in the room and all disturbing factors eliminated as far as possible.
If suitably prepared, little children also like to be involved in "playing" relaxation stories on their partners back.

The leader quietly tells the group the following story and, kneeling down next to a child, she demonstrates the massaging movements.

A child lies down on a soft mat with his/her partner kneeling beside him/her.

For a long time now, we've wanted a pet, but without being able to decide which sort of animal. But, one day, on the way to the pet shop, we were convinced we would find the right one there.

The partner's fingers move swiftly from the shoulders right across the back to his/her bottom.

Having arrived in the shop, we have a good look round at all the animals in their cages.

Move your fingers backwards and forwards across the pelvic vertebrae.

There were fishes swimming peacefully round their aquarium, ...

Stroke the palm of your hand across your partner's back.

... little monkeys doing gymnastics all over the place...

Roll the sides of your hands across the back, hopping about with the palms of your hands.

...and sweet little dwarf rabbits, snuggling close together, and so small that they would fit into your hand.

Press the fingertips of both hands close together.

Phew! It was really difficult to make a decision.

After careful thought, we decided to try a little bird – a blue and white budgie, which was very, very tame and looked as if he would suit our family just fine. We called him Florian and at the way home, he hopped about happily in front of us on his little feet.

Make light hopping movements with your fingers on your partner's back from bottom to shoulders.

Once we'd got home, we put him in a cage with bird sand on the floor.

Tap your fingers lightly on your partner's back.

We soon noticed that Florian most enjoyed scratching around wildly in his sand, scattering it all over the place.

Try and imitate scratching movements like a bird's feet on your partner's back.

Florian wasn't stupid! When we came to his cage next morning, it was empty. The bird had opened it with his beak and had flown away.

Pinch your partner's bottom gently and then let your hands flutter gently across his/her back, a tiny distance away, so that he/she only feel the air moving.

We decided to go back to the pet shop and get a new animal.

Run your fingers again down your partner's back as far as his/her bottom.

"No problem", said the pet-shop man, "go and choose yourselves another animal." We had a look round and decided on a big, fat dog lying cosily in his kennel, who looked at us trustingly.
"We'll take him", we said. "Bello is snugly and cuddly and definitely not such a mess-maker as that budgie." And so we paid for him at the till.

Count out money on your partner's back.

Bello co-operated as we put him on his lead, after which he trotted home beside us.

"Run" the palms of your hands across your partner's back and apply a bit of pressure.

Bello was a real snugly bear. He would creep up quietly…

Push the palms of your hands across his/her back.

…put his full weight on us…

Apply pressure to his/her back with your palms.

…and then nudge us with his wet nose, as if trying to say: "Come for a romp with me."

Push your knuckles gently into various points on his/her back.

What fun it was having a wild playtime with Bello! Things really began to happen! Bello took great leaps through the air and showed us all his tricks with great enthusiasm.

Using your hands alternately, put them flat for different lengths of time on arms, legs, back and head.

What we liked doing most was running both our hands through his shaggy fur and fondling him.

Keeping your hands flat, make circling movements on your partner's back, then using your fingertips stroke and fondle his/her hair.

There you are – you can see we've chosen the right animal with Bello. He suits us and we'll have a lot of fun with him. Next time we go into town, we'll call in at the pet-shop and tell the man how happy we are with him.

STORIES TO MOVE TO

When dealing with pre-school children, we pack a lot of moving exercises into little stories so that we get into their imaginary world more easily. For example, I'm sure anyone can quickly see that we get on better with an expression like "move around like giants", than if we say "stretch both arms up in the air and move forward on tip-toe with big strides." To help you put more and more of our movement stories into practice, we should like to clarify a few basic points for you.

Keep Moving

How to use the stories to move to

We haven't the slightest intention of confining you to one of our prescribed stories, or giving you the impression that the exercise leader must read the text or learn it by heart. Quite the opposite!

Our stories should reflect the needs of your particular group and so you need to ask yourselves whether the contents and progression of a story suit your group (i.e. the age of the children, the social structure of the group, your particular surroundings, etc.).

The stories work best if you tell them in your own words as part of your own experience. If the narrator really gets inside the story, living it as he/she goes, his/her tone of voice and volume will go on a long way to creating tension and thus motivate the little listeners.

It's also important to leave plenty of time for the children to carry out their movement ideas in between each pause in the story.

Sometimes, you'll find it necessary to repeat certain passages in the story or explain them in a different way. For children of about 2 years of age, you may have to "translate" a story several times, until you find the best way of getting them to do the right movements.

Finally – most important: bring the children's own ideas and comments into your story! Nobody will mind too much if the exercise leader doesn't always know how a mole shouts or a worm dances (we don't know either).

It is, however, of utmost importance that we take the children's suggestions seriously and go on encouraging them to "write" their own moving stories. This promotes the development of their imagination, self-confidence and feeling of self-worth.

AN EXCURSION INTO THE MEADOW

"It's summer! The sun's shining in, so let's get out of the house and into the fresh air where we can move about. It's super that you all want to come with me, and I promise you that we'll have a great time together out in the countryside. Our first destination is a ways from here and so we need to go a little way by car. You can all take a steering wheel in both hands and turn on the engine."

Each child grabs hold of a ring with both hands, whereby smaller children might need some help from the exercise leader. Bigger children can already drive themselves.

"There's still quite a lot of traffic around here, so we must be careful not to have an accident."

All the children weave in and out of each other watching the traffic.

"**STOP!** All the traffic lights are red."

The children stop immediately and wait impatiently for them to turn green. "Now it's amber, now its .....green!"
The journey continues.

"We've finally got to a country road, where we can put our foot down and sweep round corners."

Everyone speeds up and drives in a straight line as well as round corners round the hall.

"Stop! We've reached our destination and we're now going to back into the car park."

Look backwards and then drive backwards.

"I wonder what sort of an adventure is waiting for us round the corner. Look over there at that lovely green meadow. I'm sure that's a super place for you to all leap and jump about."

Keeping the rings in their hands, all the children run round the hall.

"Oops, we seem to have struck a particularly wet bit of ground. There are lots and lots of puddles in the meadow."

The children spread their rings out round the room to make lots of puddles.

"I'll bet it's very wet round all the puddles; let's see how we can walk across such swampy ground."

The children walk round their rings and sink up to their ankles in mud.

„Now look how muddy our shoes have got! We'd better give our feet a good shake to get all the mud off."

Shake your feet in all directions.

"Now let's take a closer look at the puddles. It looks as if there's clean water in them -that's a great opportunity to splash each other."

Splash into the "water" and flick the water with your finger; fill both hands with water and splash it over other children.

"The splashing has made us all nice and wet, but it doesn't matter any more because, now we're going to run through the puddles..."

Run from one ring to the next, but use small, quick steps to cross the rings.

"...or jump into the rings".

Final jumps into the rings.

"Phew –we're now worn out with all our jumping, so let's have a thought about all the creatures living in such a wet meadow: worms, birds, beetles, mosquitoes, flies; in fact there's a huge group of little creatures teeming about in the green grass."

The animals are shown one after the other in mime.

"Frogs feel particularly at home here and I'm sure you know how a frog jumps."

All the children hop and croak like frogs.

"Yes, and where we find frogs, we'll also find those long-legged black and white birds with their long beaks. That's right –storks! So let's walk around like storks rattling our beaks as we go. What about singing a song about frogs and storks together?"

What would you do if a stork suddenly came into the meadow, and the frogs hopped away in panic? Let's try it –you're the frogs and I'll be the stork."

The exercise leader plays the stork and the children hop away from her escaping into the corners of the hall (you could swap roles).

"Hello, my little friends. Now we've been away long enough and it's time to run to our parked cars and get ourselves home as quickly as possible."

The children grasp their rings and drive home holding their steering wheels the same way that they came.

Come on – we're off on an excursion!

If you want to play going into the garden, or going on an excursion into the meadows and woods, you only need a few mats or blankets and several chairs or little boxes plus a great deal of imagination.

In the garden:
The group leader tells the story: "Today you can look forward to our super excursion where we'll gradually get to know our immediate surroundings and then go a bit further away."

The children move around the room possibly to some suitable music.

"We'll go out through the big gate."

Two children take each other's hands and make a big gate for all the others to walk through.

"Oh, no, we haven't got the garden ready yet; can you all help me make the flowerbeds, please."

All the children fetch mats or blankets and put them on the ground.

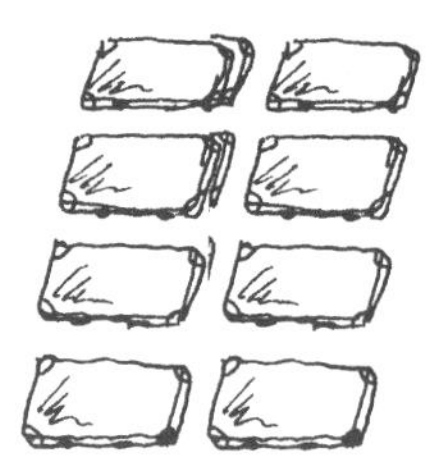

It's not easy to arrange the flowerbeds properly; have you any other ideas for the layout of our garden?

The children sort out their ideas and rearrange the mats and blankets.

"Good –that's great. Now our garden is beginning to look a bit more like a garden. Lets take a look at it from each side and run around the beds."

The children run or hop in slalom style or in large circles.

"Hey, look –here come the animals to have a look at our new garden layout. They run, crawl, creep and fly round the beds or straight into them."

The children make suggestions about which animals can come into the garden and then imitate how they move about.

"But we also want to put some plants into our vegetable and flower beds for which we'll need some little groups of workers whose job it is to make the beds look nice."

Each little group plants out its bed as they choose. Some children lie on the ground like strawberry plants, some roll up in the bed like lettuces, some are big sunflowers or swaying willows.

"Wherever you find plants flourishing you'll also find worms, ants, snails, slugs and bees."

Half of each group remains upright as plants, and the others creep, fly or crawl round them.

In the meadow:
"Now lets leave our plants growing in peace, they don't need any further attention from us. Let's stomp off through the long grass to another meadow, where we'll soon reach a fence."

The children march off to fetch some chairs or little boxes, which they put on the mats or blankets.

"Maybe some cattle or wild horses are waiting to attack us in this meadow, so let's hide first of all behind the fence."

The children try to hide behind the chairs and boxes.

"I've a sort of feeling the fence isn't solid enough.
Let's build it again and make a gate."

The children put the chairs down to make a circle with an opening in it. The mats stay inside the fence.

"Now we can see something! There are sheep inside the fence looking for food."

Virtually all the children come into the circle, but a few stay outside to guard the bleating sheep.

"Keep a careful lookout, because sheep have the habit of breaking out of unfenced land. If so, these animals must be caught again and brought straight back."

The children keep on breaking out of the circle, only to be caught and brought back again by their "keepers".

"Now we've had enough of chasing sheep. They can do what they like. Lets try again and see how many ways we can find to get over the fence."

The children climb over the chairs, crawl underneath them, walk across the seats from one chair to another.

"Well done! Now show us everything you can do with the soft meadow ground underneath you and which other animals you think live here..."

The children hop, jump, roll about, trample around and rollick across the mats, slipping into the roles of animals as they do so, e.g. a pig wallowing in the mud, a mole just rolling in and out of his molehill, horses galloping wildly around and taking sudden jumps into the air, or worms and snakes which wriggle across the ground.

"One can see that the animals don't really like being confined to the fenced-off meadow. They'd much rather be free, so, lets get rid of the fence."

The children carry the chairs to the edge.

In the wood:
"Now let's keep going, because there's a lot to do out there. A woodland area needs some new trees. A lot of little plants need setting into the ground, but the most important job is to dig a big hole, nice and deep for the plant."

The children fetch imaginary spades and dig deep holes in the ground.

"And now let's start planting."

The children play together in pairs. One child in each pair is a tree, the other the woodland worker. The "trees" are brought to each plant hole and put in the ground.

"To prevent their being knocked over by the first storm, the new trees must be stamped in well, taking care not to damage the plants."

The woodland workers stamp fiercely around their partners feet but without touching them.

"Actually there are a lot of trees still missing; the wood we've planted so far looks a bit sparsely populated. Fortunately, we've still got just as many trees left as we've already planted."

The children reverse roles and carry on playing.

"The wood is barely finished when the first animals start arriving. Let's think which animals will live in our wood."

The children suggest animals like hares, foxes, deer, owls, bears, etc. and imitate their movements.

At the pond:
"I think we'd better leave our wood with all its animals now and make our way towards that pond over there."

To make it easier for us to imagine a pond, we help the children to lay out their mats to make a sort of circle.

"Hey, look at all the things swimming around in the pond!"

Various types of water creatures are named and introduced.

"And who lives at the edge of the pond? Yes that's right –frogs and storks. I'm sure you can show us how they move."

The children march around, moving their outstretched arms up and down; they hop on all fours around the pond.

"Before we start going home, you can all jump into our pond, splash about and get each other wet."

The children plash around in imaginary water, using both hands to throw water at each other.

"I hope you're not too tired to manage the long journey home. Those who've still got enough energy to run or hop can see if they get home first."

The children move around the room, each finding his/her own comfortable walking speed.

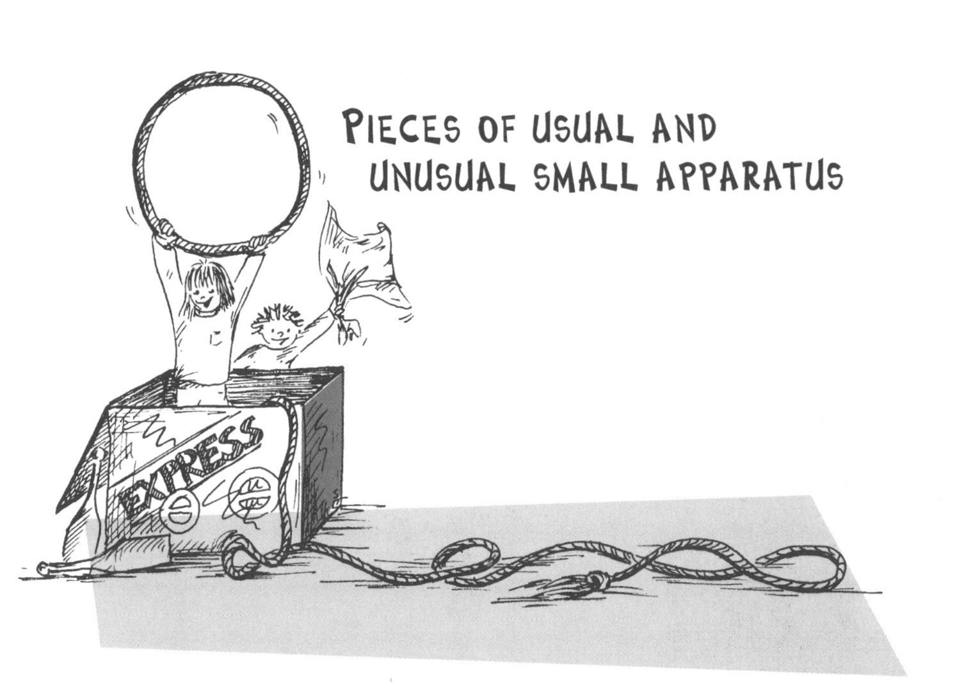

Pieces of Usual and Unusual Small Apparatus

A lot of children just sit around in their rooms at home with all too little opportunity to move about and so they are delighted when they get taken along to the sports hall.

And who takes them? Their cuddly toys which come in all sorts of different shapes and sizes! In our next gymnastics session, let's have a closer look at some of these animals, think about how they move and the children can then try to copy their movements.

You won't find that they're quiet as mice, but you'll hear a lot of squeaking, meowing, barking and roaring. If you want to, you can follow us into our sports hall zoo.

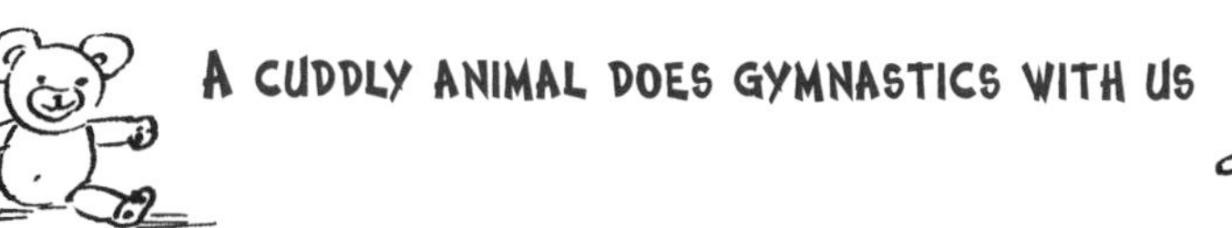

A CUDDLY ANIMAL DOES GYMNASTICS WITH US

First of all, all the animals and the children gather together in the middle of the hall and, while a welcoming song is being sung to the animals, the exercise leader sums up the various flapping and crawling animals.

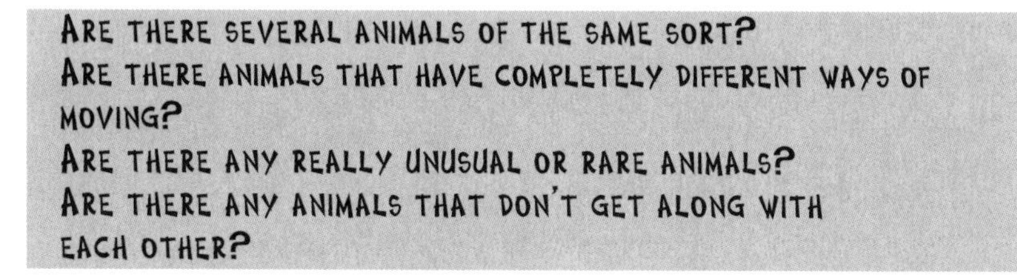

ARE THERE SEVERAL ANIMALS OF THE SAME SORT?
ARE THERE ANIMALS THAT HAVE COMPLETELY DIFFERENT WAYS OF MOVING?
ARE THERE ANY REALLY UNUSUAL OR RARE ANIMALS?
ARE THERE ANY ANIMALS THAT DON'T GET ALONG WITH EACH OTHER?

The animals are all given little name-tags, so that nobody loses one of his/her animals.

So let's introduce our favourite animals to start with:

"Hello, I'm Buzzy, Laura's bee, and who are you?
Hello, I'm Sooty, David's dog, and who are you?"

Then, everyone looks for a safe place for their animals, e.g. on a bit of carpet, in a ring, inside a box or on a mat, and they can put friendly animals down next to each other.

And now we'll play a hunting game to get to know our new sports hall zoo a bit better. All the children run round the hall and, when the music stops, the exercise leader (later the children themselves) gives them a specific task.

"Find a hopping animal."
"Could you show us how it moves?"

The animals, which the children have brought with them, give the exercise leader more and more new ideas for the hunt.
Find:

- a flying animal
- a swimming animal
- an animal which lives in the water
- an animal which lays or hides Easter eggs
- an animal which can carry its rider
- an animal which squeaks
- an animal which likes eating flies
- the smallest/biggest animal

The exercise leader can then collect further interesting ideas from the children and set them in motion.

Finally, the animals can visit each other. Individually or pairs of children can each choose an animal and carry it from one place to another.

- The smallest animals each hold paws (hands!).
- Others hover over heads or sit on shoulders.
- Special kinds of animals stand, sit or lie on their backs.
- Some are carried along squashed between your legs.
- One or two cling like crabs to your tummy.
- Some have a comfy ride in a wheelbarrow.
- Large animals can be carried together on a special seat.
- Very heavy animals will need a ring or carpet tile to be pushed or pulled from one place to another.

Suddenly, all the animals want to have a go at flying, which our exercise leader lets them do straight away. The children throw the animals to each other, but the animals are soon very tired from all this fun, so let's find them a comfy spot in the hall, like a mat or blanket and put all the cuddly animals on it.

Parachute Games or Games with a Large Sheet

Large sheets are around 6 by 6 metres and parachutes have a radius of up to 7 metres. Such massive sheets, regardless of whether they are round or square, made of parachuting silk or out of several bed sheets sown together, have an irresistible fascination for children. You can't compare the way a sheet behaves with any other sort of apparatus that we use in the sports hall. A parachute or a large sheet is communal apparatus ideal for group movement games. Not only have they both innumerable uses as small apparatus, but can also be ideally used for building caves, tunnels and hide-aways in almost any gymnastics session. In fact, any group of children should have access to such a "parachute".

The huge crawling animal:

Lay the sheet down flat on the ground.
All the children hide underneath it and then crawl together in a given direction.

The ants:

The sheet is again placed on the ground and held at each corner by four children. All the others crawl underneath it from one side to the other.

The wriggling tablecloth:

Everyone sits round the sheet with their feet hidden underneath it. Then they take hold of the edges and pull them rightly towards their tummies. By trampling fiercely underneath the sheet, they can make an otherwise smooth sheet start to flutter about. They can also try and make the fluttering start at one person and move round the circle.

It's raining:

Some of the children hold the parachute stretched out over their heads, and everyone else runs or hops about the room. When the exercise leader shouts, "it's raining", they run under cover as fast as they can.

The big umbrella:

The tallest children in the group hold the parachute stretched out over their heads and walk round the hall with it. Everyone else walks about underneath it, keeping an eye on the way it's going.

The storm:

Everyone grabs hold of a bit of the edge of the sheet. First of all, it's as quiet as a millpond and there's not a wave to be seen on the lake. Then a slight breeze starts up and the sheet begins to rustle. The wind gets stronger and stronger until it's a real hurricane. Gradually, the storm quiets down, until all is peaceful again.

We must let the air out:

Everyone swings the sheet into the air as high as possible and then pulls it down to the ground quickly, so that there's a big bubble. Then they can beat or tread on the bubble until the sheet is flat on the ground.

The flying sheet:

All the children spread out around the sheet and take hold of the edge. Then they swing the sheet evenly in big up-and-down movements. If they let go of the sheet at it's highest point, the sheet flutters through the air. Who's going to catch it?

Swapping places:

All the children grab hold of a bit of the edge of the sheet and then, from two opposite sides, swing the sheet evenly in slow up-and-down movements. The children on the two other sides swap places underneath the sheet without touching it.

The igloo:

The children swing the sheet evenly up into the air and then each child takes two steps towards the middle. Then, they bring their arms down behind their backs and sit on the edge of the sheet. This igloo is an ideal place for telling stories, playing finger puppet games or for making the igloo shake by moving your upper bodies round in a circle.

The big coach:

Some children sit down in the middle of the sheet. Three or four strong children take hold of the corners of the sheet and pull the children sitting down in their "coach" along the hall. Obviously all the children can have a ride in the coach.

Heads out of the way:

Most of the children sit in the middle of the hall on the floor and then some of them run with the sheet from one side of the hall to the other and let it float behind them at waist height. The children left sitting on the floor must lie down flat when the fluttering sheet comes over them.

The fat sausage:

If you roll the sheet up to look like a flat sausage, it can then be used for a tug-of-war or a jumping hurdle.

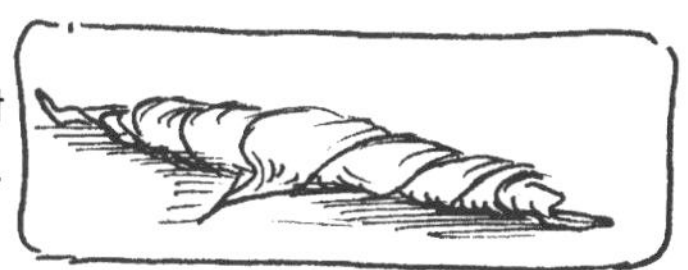

You can easily create a few more interesting games by using
small objects like balloons, soft balls, blow-up plastic balls or clothes pegs.

Dancing on the waves:

Several blown-up balloons or soft balls are placed on the sheet, and then the group tries to hurl them higher and higher into the air with the sheet. Variation: To get the objects out of the sheet by making the waves as big as possible.

From you to me:

The group holds the sheet stretched with one ball on it. This ball should then:

1. Roll around the edge of the sheet without falling off.
2. Roll diagonally from one corner to the other.
3. Take the shortest rolling route from one named child to another.

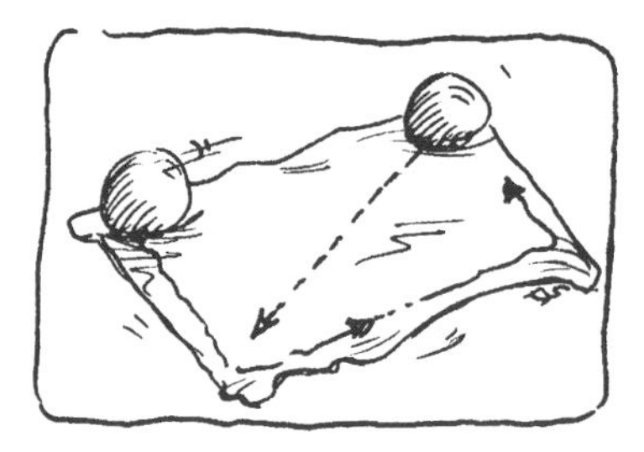

Running after it:

Two balls are placed at opposite corners of the sheet. They should then roll round evenly, remaining the same distance apart.

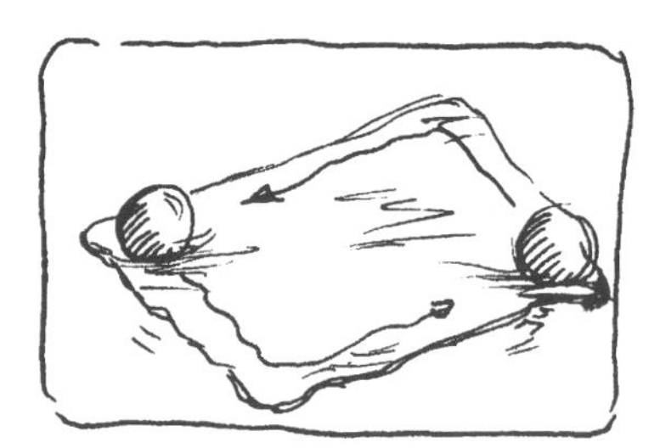

The running gate:

4 children take hold of the sheet at each corner and run up and down the hall with it. Everyone else stands around the sides of the hall and tries from there to throw balls or other small soft objects into the sheet.

The roundabout:

Everyone takes hold of the edges of the sheet with their right hand and the roundabout is set in motion with the following rhyme: "Slowly, slowly, round and round; Rushing, rushing, on we go, Our roundabout's now off the ground. Till we slow down once again, And – STOP." So that nobody gets dizzy, swap over to holding the sheet with your left hand, so that the roundabout turns the other way.

Catching mosquitoes:

Everyone holds onto the sheet with one hand and shakes it up and down. The "spare" hand can catch mosquitoes that the exercise leader throws into the sheet as sweets or little balloons. The sheet is shaken for as long as it takes everyone to catch a mosquito, after which the spare mosquitoes are collected up off the ground for the next game.

The small games in this book depend on the imagination and skill in the portrayal of the players. The children take their cues from pictures to get to grips with voices and movements peculiar to animals. Children slip happily and comfortably into such roles, by means of which both their imagination and creativity are challenged.

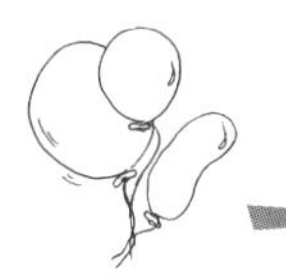

Animals — Animals — Animals

Equipment: Cards with photos or drawings of animals on them in duplicate (see our creative corner). For our younger children: familiar animals and pets whose noises and movements can be easily imitated.

Game 1:

2 children play together. All the animal pictures lie face down on the floor. One child fetches a card and tries to be the animal, so that his/her partner can guess what he/she is. Swap roles.

Game 2:

Played in the same way as the first game but silently, like a pantomime, without making any animal noises.

Game 3:

The group plays together. Each child gets a card and moves around the room to some suitable music. They can swap the animal cards as often as they like whilst moving around. When the music stops, each child looks at its card, imitates that animal and then tries to find a partner with the same animal card.

Game 4:

The same as the third game, but with the animals finding each other either from the animal noises or just from the movements.

Game 5:

Depending on the size of the group, you will need several copies of the same animal. In a group of 20, you need to divide them into 4 groups of 5 children in each. So, you'll need pictures of 5 dogs, 5 sheep, 5 frogs and 5 birds. Put the pictures face down, and then let each child take a picture and look at it without any other child seeing it. When the cue is given, everyone makes all the animal noises or all the animal movements at the same time, until the four animal families have found each other. Then the groups are given movement tasks, e.g. all the birds visit the frogs or all the dogs go and catch the sheep, etc.

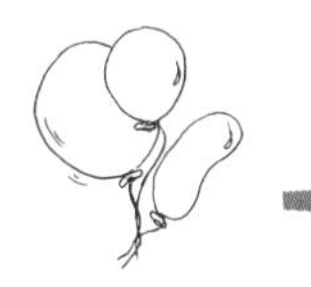

Small Games – Here for the first time:

You in the pink jumper!...
New children to our group like a bit of help with settling in. They have all sorts of new things to come to terms with, as the following story shows. We'll start in the changing rooms.
Name games help with the first stage of getting to know each other and make integration into the group easier.

Before our next session begins, there are a lot of wild things going on in the changing rooms. Wherever you look there's something scurrying, crawling or wriggling about; you can hear squeaking, laughing, moaning and whining. Sally hasn't seen her little friend Michelle for a whole week. So, first of all, they have to give each other a big hug. The fact that they have to clear a few other children out of the way to get to each other doesn't bother them at all. Johnny, Steve and Luke barely have time to let their mothers get them changed, because they'd far rather be climbing about on the new cloakroom stands. Sarah and Josie have just invented a new game called: "Throwing your shoes into the air and catching them again."

But by no means are only the children active! Mrs. Brown is telling Mrs. Newton about her last visit to the doctor's, and three other mums are standing in the corridor swapping news about the new nursery school teacher. Everyone is well and truly occupied apart from Mrs. Elson and her daughter, Lucy, who are there for the first time. It took them a long time to take this first step, but now they're standing around somewhat helpless and forlorn at the back of the changing rooms. They have a furtive look round, envying all the others who seem to have no problems with talking and moving about.

It's nearly 3 o'clock and one by one all the mothers and children leave the room to go into the sports hall.

Mrs. Elson and Lucy come last.
The sports hall is soon full of happy turmoil with children flitting about and some mothers trying to catch them, whilst others are still chatting. Mrs. Elson holds Lucy's hand tightly, as they both stand by the door and watch all the other children in amazement.

Lucy is glad that she can stay safely holding her mummy's hand, because there are so-o-o many new things going on around her and she's afraid.

At last, the exercise leader discovers the newcomers; without any further ado, she goes straight up to them and gives them a friendly welcome. She doesn't need to ask why they're standing so close together, she just knows. Obviously the exercise leader knows that:

- Little Lucy has never seen such a big, bare room before.
- She's confused by the sight of so many unknown children running about.
- She doesn't like all the noise.
- She hasn't any idea how she will fit into this group.
- She's torn between wanting to stay and going straight back home again.

However, the exercise leader knows all about such anxieties and it's good to bear in mind the following questions:

- Am I going to be accepted by the group which is already there? Will I make new contacts?

- Perhaps I'm too clumsy or not sporty enough. Will the others laugh at me?

- Will my child be able to do as much as the other children in his/her group?

The first encouraging factor is that the exercise leader knows all about these fears and reservations. By talking to her, (also before and after the session) you can get rid of any worries. She can reassure you that anyone would understand if the "newcomers" are first withdrawn and apprehensive, but there are ways of helping them to find their way into the group and get rid of their inhibitions.

Who is Who?

All the children run around the hall to music. Suddenly the music stops and the exercise leader calls someone's name. They sit down quickly on the ground just where they are. All the others form a group round him/her, clap their hands or hop around him/her. When the music starts up again, they all carry on charging about until someone else's name is called out and a new circle is formed. The game continues until all the children's names have been called.

I'll Bring You Your Name

With newly-formed groups it's best to start with a name-tag game, using sticky tape. Everyone has their name written on a label which they then stick on the wall of the sports hall. After running around to the music for a little while, everyone takes someone else's label and tries to find who it belongs to. The exercise leader can obviously help the children read the name tags. The game ends when everyone is wearing their own label.

Quiet games:

CREEPING ABOUT

The group sits around in a big circle with one child in the middle with his/her eyes shut.

The exercise leader gives another child the cue to get up very, very quietly and creep towards the child sitting in the middle (everyone else keeps very quiet).

If the child in the middle hears a noise and turns towards the approaching child, then he/she has to sit down again and another child has a go. When someone reaches the middle without being heard, he/she swaps places with the middle child.

THROUGH THE FENCE

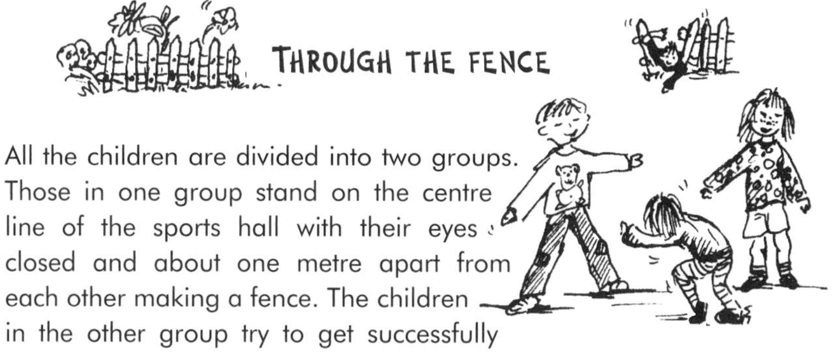

All the children are divided into two groups. Those in one group stand on the centre line of the sports hall with their eyes closed and about one metre apart from each other making a fence. The children in the other group try to get successfully from one side of the hall to the other. They do this by creeping carefully up to the fence and slipping unnoticed through a gap. During the next round, roles are reversed.

Games in an easily-manageable area:

SHOW ME YOUR HANDS

A lot of big and little boxes have been spread out all over the hall and the children start to run around the obstacles whilst music is being played. If the music stops, they all quickly hide behind the boxes, starting again when the music begins. When the music stops for the second time and they have hidden themselves, the exercise leader says: "Show me a hand" (or a thumb, your head, 2 feet, your bottom etc.).

Games for getting to know other children:

DRAWING CHILDREN TOGETHER

Using the animal pictures at the back of this book, we will try and make contact with everyone in our group. Everyone gets an animal picture, making sure that there are two of each animal in the game before you start, e.g. 2 dogs, 2 cats, 2 cows etc.

After a short time of running around to music, we ask the children to look for their "relatives". This can be done either by imitating animal noises or by pantomime movements calling out dog-dog-dog or cow-cow-cow. When all the pairs have found each other, they should carry out some task or other:

- Some children make a fence for the others to climb through or crawl under.
- Some children build a tunnel by doing high press-ups or by putting their hands together and others crawl through.
- Everyone holds hands and moves around the sports hall like a snake.
- Everyone makes a train, which sometimes goes fast, sometimes slow around the hall.
- The children hold hands and run around in a circle to the left or the right.
- Everyone crawls about on the floor catching hold of one another's hands.
- The children build a statue.

After one of the tasks has been completed, the music begins again and everyone runs about swapping animal pictures. New partners are found during the next pause in the music, and the exercise leader gives out the next task. This is a good way of constantly making new contacts, which quickly helps newcomers to feel at home.

CAT AND MOUSE

Equipment: 1 parachute or a large sheet.

Everyone takes hold of the edge of the parachute and moves it up and down in waves. A little mouse is darting about frantically under the sheet, trying not to get caught by the cat. Fortunately, the cat can't get under the sheet, as she would then be able to see the mouse and catch it.

So, she creeps or runs about on the sheet, unable to see exactly where the mouse is, because of all the wave movements. Should the cat succeed, however, in catching the little mouse, she can become the mouse and a new cat is chosen.

THE MOUSETRAP

Equipment: each pair of children needs a shoebox and a soft ball.
Game idea: the children stand in pairs next to each other (each pair with a shoebox) in the hall and when they hear "There goes the mouse!" one child from each pair rolls a ball across the room. Then the little mouse-catchers run after the mice as fast as they can, trying to catch them with the shoebox.

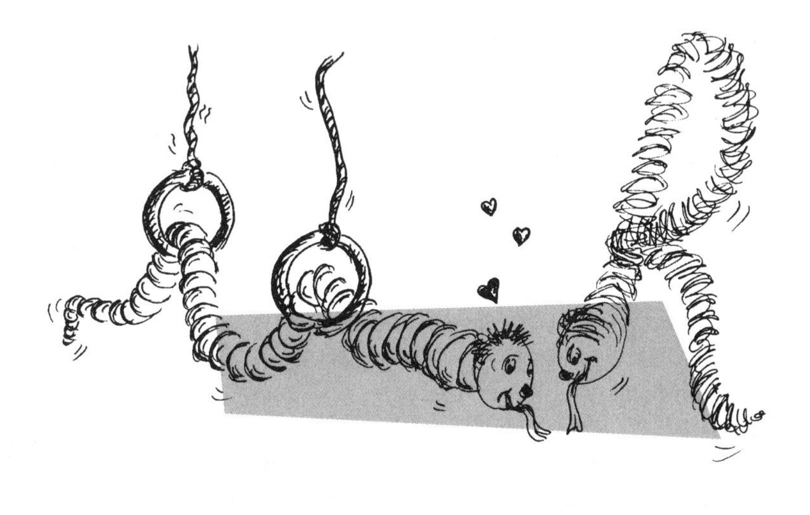

FUN ACTIVITIES

If it's warm enough outside, go outside into the fresh air! Children usually enjoy going for a walk together with a lot of other children and their parents. Of course, we won't just go for a boring walk in the woods, in the fields or in the park; no, we'll join "Mr. Wriggley", a fat caterpillar, and see how he turns into a beautiful butterfly.

AN ACTIVITIES WALK WITH MR. WRIGGLEY

Before we set this activity in motion, you need to do some careful planning and preparation.

PREPARATION:

The exercise leader needs to look for a suitable route for short and long-legged people, which can be completed in about 40 minutes. For adults this means about 20 minutes of walking time, because the activities to be inserted can quickly make it a 60-90 minute route.

The tasks to be completed must be suitable for the terrain and any other natural features. The tasks printed in the letters to parents and children by "Mr. Wriggley" may just serve as ideas, but we've already tested them carefully in various places.

It's a good idea for any additional tasks or spontaneous ideas you may have, depending on your surroundings whilst out, to have a few spare pieces of writing paper and pens.

You will also need a number of little caterpillars to mark out the route like signposts. The more caterpillars the children can find, the more exciting their walk through the woods! These little caterpillars (about 20 per person) should be made secretly at home, without the children seeing them in advance.

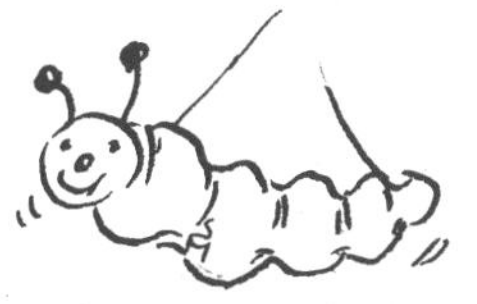

You can find instructions for making these, butterflies and other little signposts in our "Creative Corner".

Experience has taught us that there are always a few taller or particularly agile children, who like to rush on ahead leaving nothing for the smaller or slower children to find. Signposts in different colours can help here, where each age group or several families of children with similar temperaments or levels of development are given different colours, e.g. the two-year-olds the yellow ones and the older children the brown and green caterpillars, which are more difficult to find.

From our big caterpillar, "Mr. Wriggley", we keep on finding new letters evenly distributed along the path. There are all sorts of different tasks for everyone in them. The following letters, if they seem appropriate, can be copied before your walk, put into weatherproof folders and hung on trees and bushes along the side of the path. Mums and dads of the little letter-discoverers read each letter and then the whole group carries out the task together.

The exercise leader motivates using her own words and fills in the explanations, rules of the game or instructions if necessary. At the end of the walk, everyone sees the wonderful metamorphosis of "Mr. Wriggley" and his relations into butterflies: lots of butterflies are "flying" in a tree standing in an open space. They can be hung with brightly coloured ribbons from a tree or a bush.

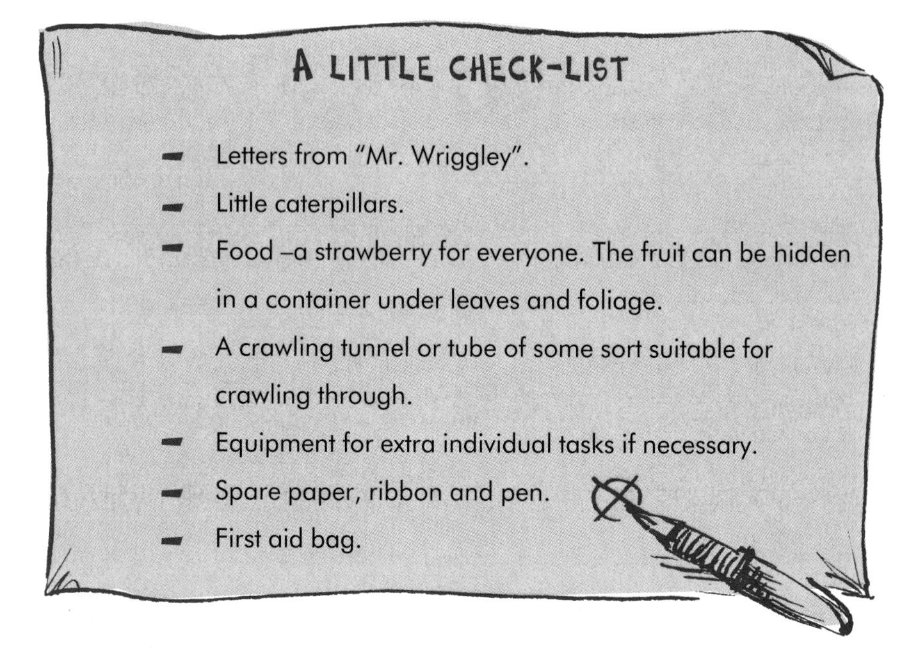

A LITTLE CHECK-LIST

- Letters from "Mr. Wriggley".
- Little caterpillars.
- Food –a strawberry for everyone. The fruit can be hidden in a container under leaves and foliage.
- A crawling tunnel or tube of some sort suitable for crawling through.
- Equipment for extra individual tasks if necessary.
- Spare paper, ribbon and pen.
- First aid bag.

Obviously everyone is responsible for ensuring that nothing is left behind in the woods. If you like, you can insert an extra task, which encourages everyone to gather up rubbish and take a wagon to help.

ON THE DAY OF THE WALK

The exercise leader and her assistant set out about an hour before the start of the walk (so that all the instructions can't be removed by other walkers).

They start at the destination by hanging up all the butterflies, and then they hang up all the letters in reverse order and space out and hide all the little caterpillars.

If there are certain places where special tasks with equipment are to be carried out, like the caterpillars' favourite food, then these must be prepared for appropriately.

Back at the start, we have a short breather and then the first children begin to arrive with their parents.

It depends on the type of group whether the exercise leader lets all the parents and children start at the same time. It might be better to form smaller groups, where the composition of the group suits the children's level of ability. The youngest start first and subsequent groups at intervals of five minutes, so that everyone reaches the butterfly tree at the same time. You can reduce the waiting time for other families starting later by playing some singing games.
Right –we're ready to start and wish you lots of fun with "Mr. Wriggley!"

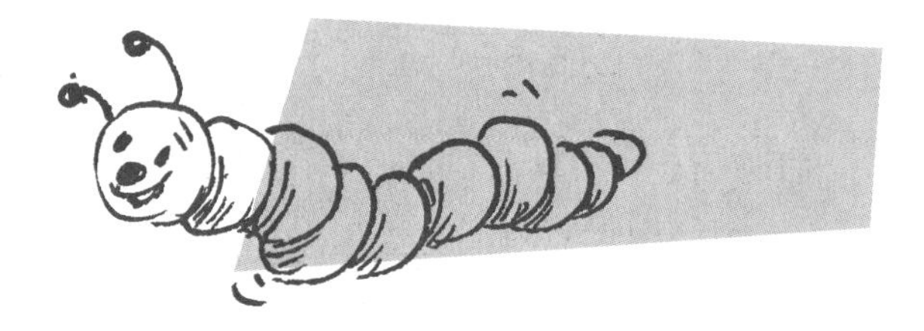

DEAR CHILDREN, DEAR PARENTS

Please let me introduce myself.

My name is Mr. Wriggley and I'm a caterpillar, who's just longing to turn into a beautiful butterfly. You see, it's like this for us butterfly caterpillars. We all crawl out of a little egg as tiny little caterpillar babies and we then have to stuff ourselves with lots and lots of leaves so that we grow quickly. When we're big enough, we have a rest and then turn into a butterfly. On your way through the wood, you can shorten the waiting time for me a bit, so that it's very likely that we can all see me change into a butterfly today. Just follow the trail, which my little caterpillar friends have laid for you.

I wish you a lot of fun on the way.
Yours, Mr. Wriggley.

Hello, my lovelies,

Here I am again!

Have you ever played hide-and-seek in the woods? Sometimes I play that with my friends. Tell your mummies to shut their eyes tightly.

Then look for a good hiding place behind a big tree or in some bushes. Your mummies must take a long time finding you!

On your marks-get set-go!

See you later.
Yours, Mr. Wriggley.

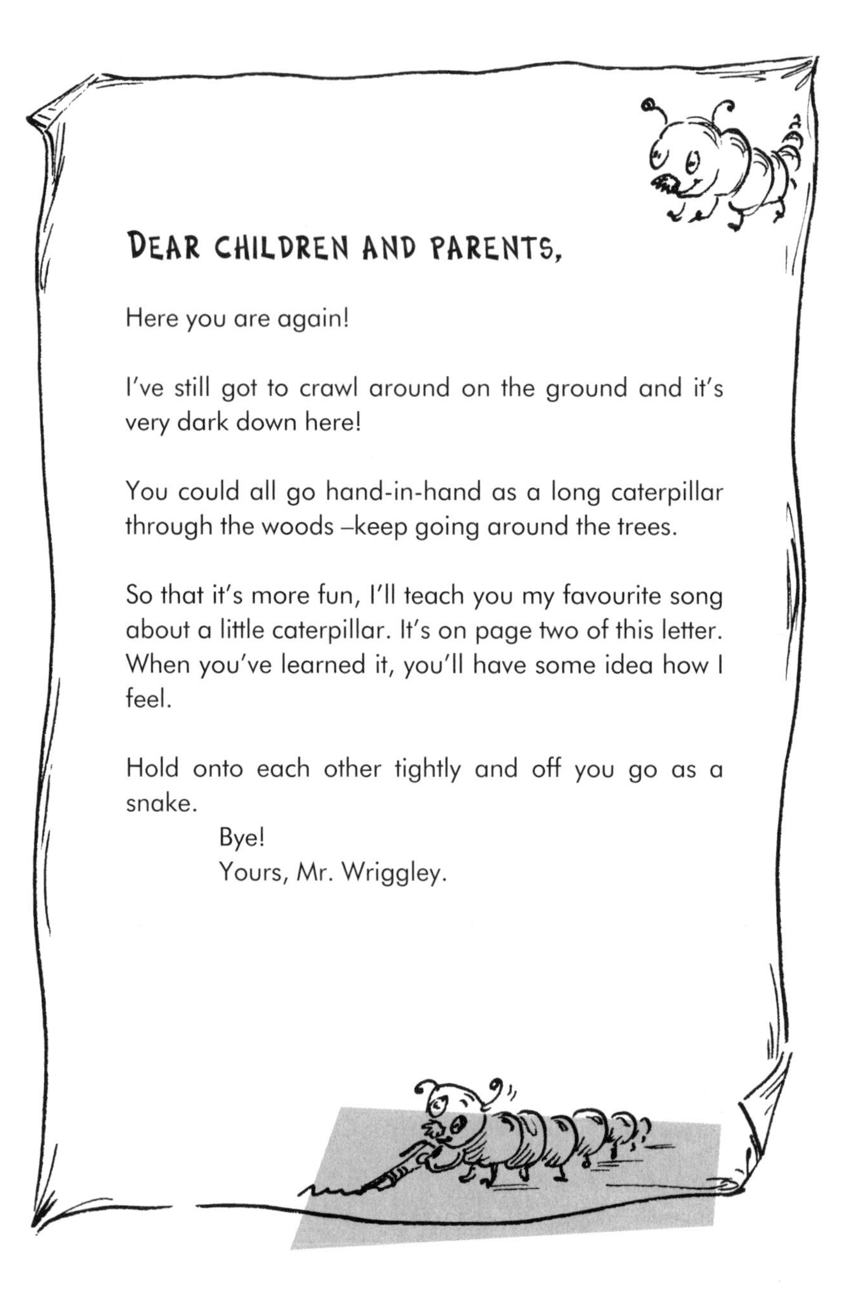

DEAR CHILDREN AND PARENTS,

Here you are again!

I've still got to crawl around on the ground and it's very dark down here!

You could all go hand-in-hand as a long caterpillar through the woods –keep going around the trees.

So that it's more fun, I'll teach you my favourite song about a little caterpillar. It's on page two of this letter. When you've learned it, you'll have some idea how I feel.

Hold onto each other tightly and off you go as a snake.

Bye!
Yours, Mr. Wriggley.

THE LITTLE CATERPILLAR

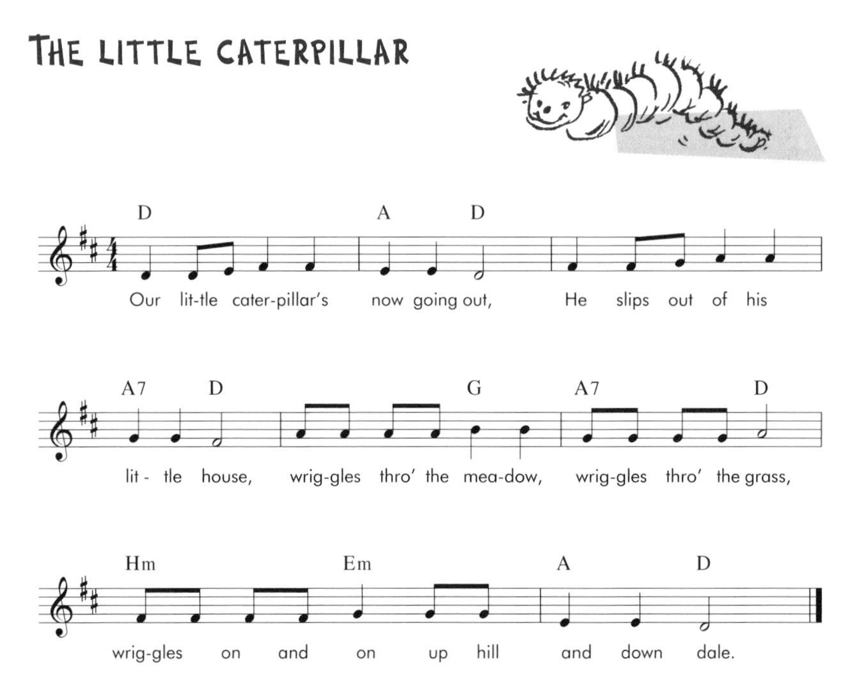

Our little caterpillar's now going out,
he slips out of his little house,
wriggles thro' the meadow, wriggles thro' the grass,
wriggles on and on up hill and down dale.

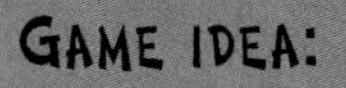

Everyone holds onto each other and moves like a long caterpillar around all the trees, bushes, flowers, grass etc.

HELLO,

I'm still a caterpillar and would like to fly so-o-o much!

I'm sure one gets along faster that way! Perhaps all you parents and children could show me how.

So go for a good run as fast as you can!

Bye for now,
Mr. Wriggley.

Hello-o,
Here I am again, poor worm that I am!

It's a nice fine day today, but can you imagine how uncomfortable it is here when it's raining?

Then I'd just love to have a little house to creep into. Hey, I've had an idea. What about you're building me a little house of branches, leaves and grass; would you like to?

Also, if you wish, you could build a house out of big branches for your family and friends.

Thanks,
Mr. Wriggley.

WELL, CHILDREN!

Would you like to try a caterpillar's favourite food?

It's buried around here somewhere, so spread out and look for it, but be careful that you don't tread on it.

If you find it, you can eat it. I hope you didn't get to fat. Now try and crawl through this.

You know now what it feels like to have to struggle to nibble your way through your food.

Well –see you again soon,
Mr. Wriggley.

WELL, MY FRIENDS!

Now that I'm full, I really must have a sleep.

Please creep through the next bit really quietly, so that you don't wake my friends up.

Thanks,
Mr. Wriggley.

HELLO FRIENDS,

Now watch very carefully. All eyes and everyone lined up behind each other. Keep close together, because we're coming to a dangerous bit of crawling.

Yours,
Mr. Wriggley.

HELLO FRIENDS,

Well, that's surprised you, hasn't it?

We've all come together here and found that it's not as easy as it looks to change into a butterfly.

Perhaps you could help us a bit. Pick one of us up carefully in one hand and tweak its tail carefully with the other hand....

The wings are opening slowly....
It's spreading them out....
And flying, flying, flying, ...

Have a good flight 'til we meet again.

Yours,
Mr. Wriggley

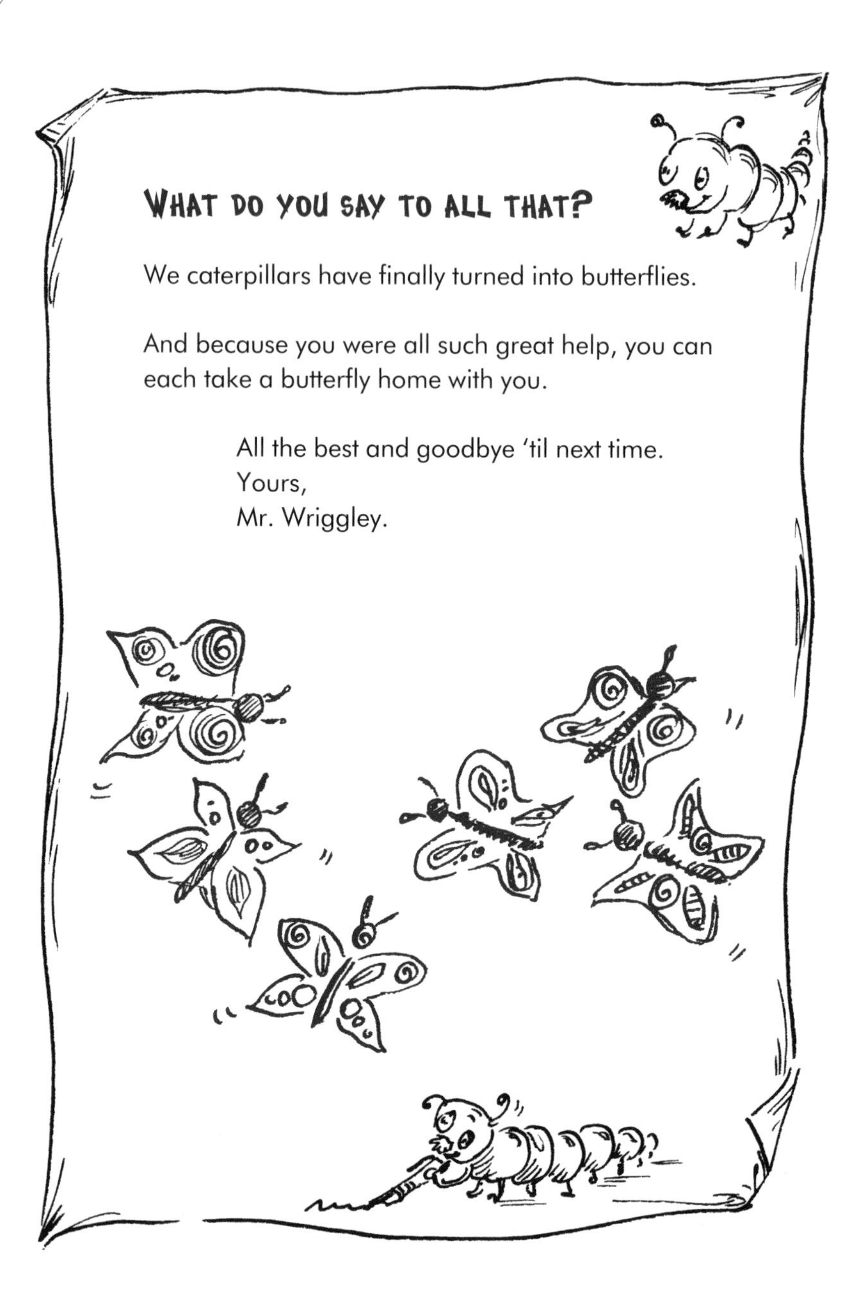

WHAT DO YOU SAY TO ALL THAT?

We caterpillars have finally turned into butterflies.

And because you were all such great help, you can each take a butterfly home with you.

All the best and goodbye 'til next time.
Yours,
Mr. Wriggley.

HELLO, THERE YOU ARE AGAIN!

CREATIVE
CORNER

MR. WRIGGLEY, THE FAT CATERPILLAR

1. 4 circles with a radius of about 7 cm are cut out of green cardboard and a similar sized circle is cut out of thick red paper.
2. The green circles used for the body overlap each other by about a 1/3 and are stuck (at about 80°) with the red head above them.
3. Eyes and mouth are painted on and then two feelers of about 4 cm long and 0.3 cm wide complete your caterpillar.

Little caterpillars of various colours form the signposts for the nature walk, and you can cut them out from the patterns given below.

BUTTERFLIES 1-2-3

1. A toilet paper roll is painted green to make the body or wrapped in green paper. Pipe cleaners are poked through at one end as feelers and the eyes either painted or stuck on. A length of coloured ribbon is pulled through the roll and knotted. Finally, a coloured chiffon scarf is stuffed into the roll, so that only a little bit is peeping out as a tail. Once at home, the children themselves have got wings with the chiffon scarf, as well as a new toy for throwing, catching and juggling with. The naked little caterpillar can be hung up somewhere to keep things in their bedroom.

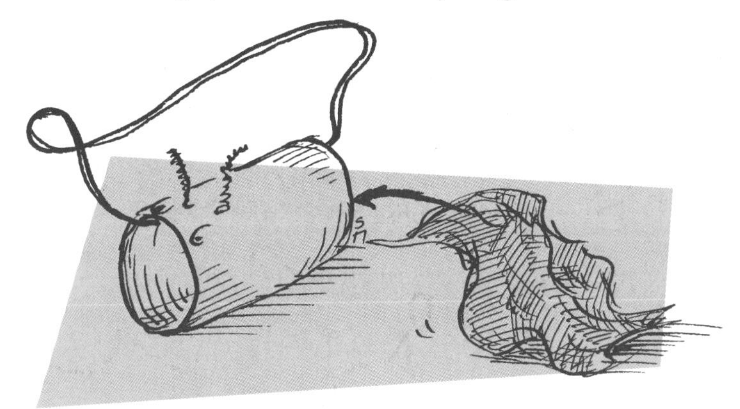

These butterflies are made out of wooden clothes pegs and a serviette or crêpe paper or left-overs from wrapping paper.

You can enlarge the pattern for this butterfly and make it first out of cardboard. Then this can be used to make lots of butterflies out of different coloured card, sticking a sweet in the middle of each one as a little surprise.

copy model

Animal cards

copy model

copy model

A LOOK AT THE AUTHORS:

Heidi Lindner:
Heidi Lindner, editor and authoress of the practical series "Let's Move", has been involved for many years in both the education and continuing education of exercise leaders, educators and junior school teachers for various employers. She founded the "Pipo Learner's Workshop" and, as Rolf Zuckowski's tour leader, she set up many new projects and events for and with children; for example, the children's gymnastics show "Star children".

Gisela Stein:
Gisela Stein works throughout Germany and Austria as an exercise leader and lecturer for education and continuing education in the areas of parent-child and children's gymnastics. For a long time, her work has involved her in producing a well-qualified, varied and imaginative exercise programme for pre- and infant/junior school children.

Silke Mehler:
Silke Mehler is a qualified psychologist and psychotherapist. For 11 years she has been in charge of the illustrations for the "Pipo Learner's Workshop" and the "Let's Move" books , in which she incorporates her experience from working as an exercise leader and lecturer with children and young people.